IELTS General Writing Task Masterclass ®

IELTS Writing Task 1 & IELTS Writing Task 2

Marc Roche

www.idmadrid.es

Copyright © 2018 **Marc Roche**

Contents

About This Book

The writing part of the IELTS test is often quite confusing for candidates. "IELTS General Writing Task Masterclass" by Marc Roche and IDM Business & Law ®, is a complete IELTS preparation self-study book, which focuses on practical English writing skills for the official IELTS exam. This is an excellent book for preparing the IELTS Writing Task 1 & IELTS Writing Task 2 within the IELTS General Training exam.

You will be shown step-by-step, how to answer the different questions and avoid the most common mistakes in the exam, through a series of easy to follow instructions, exercises and examples. By the end of this book, you will know how to achieve outstanding results in IELTS Writing Task 1 & IELTS Writing Task 2.

"IELTS General Writing Task Masterclass ®" from the IELTS Writing Masterclass series, is perfect for Upper-Intermediate and Advanced students, and it is based on years of real classroom experience and years of research into second language writing skills acquisition. It contains IELTS writing exercises and specialised IELTS exam strategies to quickly improve your IELTS General Test results.

The 12 Rules of IELTS General Writing

1. Use correct spellings.

2. Avoid contractions like we're; use we are.

3. Never use 'slang' words like 'gonna'.

4. Use formal English words, such as 'discuss' rather than 'chat'.

5. Use correct punctuation: avoid very long sentences.

6. Write a mixture of short and longer (complex) sentences.

7. Use your own words, or give a clear reference to the source.

8. Write so that the reader understands exactly what you mean.

9. Connect your ideas clearly (e.g. Finally/In conclusion/However)

10. Use correct grammar that makes your meaning clear.

11. Do not write informally or in a very friendly way

12. Only give true data; do not invent or change it.

IELTS General Writing Overview

Length: 60 minutes

General Writing Test

Task	Word count	Advised Timing	Task description
1	150	20 mins	The candidate is presented with a situation and is asked to write a letter requesting information, or explaining an issue. The letter may be personal, semi-formal or formal in style.
2	250	40 mins	Presenting arguments and opinions in a discursive essay about a topical issue.

TIP: The exam says to write a 'minimum of 150/250 words but don't write much more. Aim for 10 or 20 words more at the most.

IELTS General

The Writing component of IELTS General includes two tasks. Topics are of general interest to, and suitable for candidates entering work and postgraduate studies or seeking professional registration.

Task 1

You will be presented with a problem or an issue and asked to describe, summarise, or explain the information in your own words. You may be asked to write a letter of application, a letter of recommendation, a letter concerning accommodation or a letter of complaint or which explains the problems with something among other possibilities.

Task 2

You will be asked to write an essay in response to a point of view, argument or problem. Responses to both tasks must be in a formal style.

Chapter 1:

Formal Letters in English

In this section we are going to examine the formal letter tasks in the IELTS General Training exam.

IDENTIFYING KEY INFORMATION

Firstly, we will practice identifying key information in the question. Next, we will suggest ways you can organize formal letters, and then we will look at the kind of language you should be using. Finally, we practice useful language, grammar and vocabulary, which are essential and will help you gain lots of marks in the exam.

We will examine two types of formal letter or email: the letter of reference and the letter of application. These aren't the only types of formal letter or email you might be asked to write about in the exam but they will serve as perfect examples here.

LETTER OF REFERENCE

In this type of formal letter, you're asked to provide a reference for a colleague or friend to a prospective employer or educational institution.

You may find it helpful to note down useful expressions which you can include,

Some Useful Language for this type of letter or email

I have known X for ….

I am confident that ….

I have no hesitation in recommending him ….

X is sociable, reliable, self-confident, outgoing

X possesses a thorough grounding in …

stand him in good stead

as is shown by the fact that …

As you may know, your writing will be assessed in terms of:

- Task Achievement
- Coherence and Cohesion
- Lexical Resource
- Grammatical Range and Accuracy

Including all the relevant content in your letter and presenting it clearly will contribute hugely towards you scoring well as the target reader will be fully informed.

Candidates often lose marks in the exam, either because they have included irrelevant information, perhaps they've forgotten to include something important, or they've misinterpreted the question.

Here is a typical example of a formal letter question. We will practice identifying key content in order to avoid losing marks. We'll work through the task chronologically.

Read the example and answer the following question.

1. What is the first key piece of information you need to refer to in your answer?

A friend of yours is applying for a job in a popular shop, as a retail shop assistant for English speaking tourists visiting your city. The shop has asked you to provide a character reference for your friend.

The reference should indicate

- how long you have known each other.
- It must include a detailed description of the person's character
- the reason why he or she would be suitable for the job.

Write at least 150 words

This seems like an obvious question but it's vital to have it very clear in your mind that <u>they are asking you to write a reference</u>. Firstly, this indicates that we need to be thinking about a formal register and it also helps us to start the letter.

For example:

"To whom it may concern,

Mary and I have been working together at J&J Retail for 10 years.

. . . ."

2. What is the next important information?

We need to pay attention to the type of job we are writing the reference for. The job in this case is a retail assistant for a popular shop. It is important to remember that the information we provide must be relevant for this position.

3. What qualities or skills does a suitable candidate for almost any job need to have?

You can use the following ideas for any job reference.

i. Personal and social skills (people skills/inter-personal abilities): The successful candidate will need to have good personal and social skills so we must emphasise the person's personal and social skills in the context of their application.

ii. English language skills: we must emphasise his or her English language skills, as all jobs that you will be asked to write references for in this exam will require the candidate to speak good English to communicate with customers, clients, tourists, guests etc…

iii. Time-management ability is another skill that every person needs for a job, so regardless of the job that they present you with, you can talk about this.

4. So what's next?

Previous experience. We need to mention any relevant work the person has done in the past that will support their application. Again, we could link this with the earlier part about their people skills or about their time-management skills.

We need to show the person is suitable for the post, but this doesn't necessarily need to be in a separate paragraph. You can write about their experience in the same paragraph whilst you describe their character and skills.

Alternatively, it could be something you include at the end of the letter but either way, you always need to emphasize the person's suitability for the post.

ORGANIZATION (REFERENCE AND APPLICATION):

Read the example again and answer the following questions.

1. How many paragraphs would you have?

2. Which paragraphs would deal with which issues?

Example Question

A friend of yours is applying for a job in a popular shop, as a retail shop assistant for English speaking tourists visiting your city. The shop has asked you to provide a character reference for your friend.

The reference should indicate

- how long you have known each other.

- It must include a detailed description of the person's character

- the reason why he or she would be suitable for the job.

Write at least 150 words

One idea is to organise this around two or three content paragraphs along with an opening and closing paragraph, so four or five paragraphs in total.

Paragraph 1

The first paragraph is obviously going to deal with our reason for writing. In this case, to write a reference for a friend (or in the letter of application to apply for something). In a letter of reference or a letter of application, the first main content paragraph usually outlines the person's skills and experience, perhaps including any relevant qualifications they might have.

Paragraph 2

Then, we could move on to look at the person's character and their personal qualities.

We could deal with our friend's suitability for the post in these two paragraphs if we wanted to or we could choose to have a third content paragraph where we emphasize the person's strengths once again.

Finally, we would end the letter with a closing remark such as

"Please do not hesitate to contact me if you have any questions. "

Organizing your paragraphs in a logical way like this, would make the letter coherent overall and it would give the reader a visual guide to your organization especially if you leave a line or a space between each paragraph. It would also help you deal with the main sections of the letter in a logical order.

Expressing Ideas:

But what about how you express ideas within paragraphs? How can you link ideas in and between sentences? Let's look at some of the ways you can do this.

Linking Words:

The first method are straightforward linking words that you've probably used in your writing for a while. Words or expressions like firstly or in addition, or for instance. These enable you to link ideas simply and effectively.

Discourse Markers:

The assessment criteria often refers to discourse markers. These are just slightly higher level linking words or expressions such as moreover, furthermore or by way of example.

Exercise 1:

Look at the gaps in sample answer below:

Where could you use these linking words and discourse markers to complete the text? You will not need to sue all of them.

Firstly, in addition, for instance, moreover, furthermore or by way of example.

<u>**Sample Answer (Letter of Reference):**</u>

To whom it may concern,

Mary and I worked together at J&J Retail for 10 years.
It is my pleasure to recommend her for the position of shop assistant.

1......................., Mary is a self-confident and outgoing person, who finds it easy to relate to people from all kinds of backgrounds.

During her time at J&J Retail, Mary proved to be friendly, communicative, hard-working and excellent at managing her time. 2...................., Mary is the kind of person who works well with others, as she displays great sensitivity and sympathy. She was always willing to contribute and help her colleagues. 3.................... at J&J Retail she was popular and fully committed to the organisation's objectives.

4.................... at J&J Retail, Mary demonstrated excellent English language skills dealing with English-speaking customers on a daily basis. She passed her English exams around 6 months ago and has a keen interest in fashion, which I am sure will stand her in good stead when she is helping customers in English.

I recommend Mary without reservation — she would be an excellent asset to your company.

Please do not hesitate to contact me if you have any questions.

Sincerely,

Your name and Surname

Now you can check your answers by reading "Sample Answer (Letter of Reference)" on the next page...

Sample Answer (Letter of Reference):

To whom it may concern,

Mary and I worked together at J&J Retail for 10 years.

It is my pleasure to recommend her for the position of shop assistant.

Firstly, Mary is a self-confident and outgoing person, who finds it easy to relate to people from all kinds of backgrounds.

During her time at J&J Retail, Mary proved to be friendly, communicative, hard-working and excellent at managing her time. In addition, Mary is the kind of person who works well with others, as she displays great sensitivity and sympathy. She was always willing to contribute and help her colleagues. Moreover, (Furthermore) at J&J Retail she was popular and fully committed to the organisation's objectives.

By way of example, (For instance) at J&J Retail, Mary demonstrated excellent English language skills dealing with English-speaking customers on a daily basis. She passed her English exams around 6 months ago and has a keen interest in fashion, which I am sure will stand her in good stead when she is helping customers in English.

I recommend Mary without reservation — she would be an excellent asset to your company.

Please do not hesitate to contact me if you have any questions.

Sincerely,

Your name and Surname

(Word count: 197)

Well done if you answered correctly, but be careful when you write, as there is always the danger that you can overuse devices like these. This makes your writing seem unnatural and demonstrates to the examiner that you do not really understand how to use them. To avoid this issue, let's look at some other cohesive devices you can use to help you organize your ideas.

Reference pronouns:

Reference pronouns like this, that, they or it are commonly used to refer back to something or someone recently mentioned.

Relative clauses:

Relative clauses can be used to give added information to a statement and they allow you to link ideas together in well-formed sentences.

Substitution:

Other forms of cohesive devices include things like substitution. This is where you use a synonym for example to refer backwards or forwards to a connected point in the text.

E.g. Replacing a verb phrase:

The management team at J & J Retails were very happy with Mary, and so were the rest of the staff (and the rest of the staff were also very happy with her).

Using paragraphs and a variety of cohesive devices effectively will help you score well in the "Coherence and Cohesion" and "Task achievement" parts of the assessment criteria. **Tip:** When you're reading, make a point of looking out for cohesive devices like the ones we've looked at in this section.

LETTER OF APPLICATION

In this type of formal letter, you're asked to write a formal letter or email applying for a job, accommodation or place on a course. Again, the recipient of this letter is a prospective employer or educational institution.

Cover letters, sometimes called letters of application, are a very important part of your application, whether you're a student at university or a candidate looking for a job. While there are virtually no limits to the different designs you can use for your letter of application, there are some general guidelines you will want to apply to make sure it is appropriate for the exam. It is first important to make sure your cover letter has an excellent appearance in terms of both structure and language.

Make sure you learn the name of the person or organization that you're writing if they appear in the instructions. The name must always be spelled correctly.

The next thing you want to do is to demonstrate your qualifications for the job. It is best to write two powerful sentences explaining why you have the necessary skills to perform the job you are interested in. After this, you will want to let the potential employer know that your resume is enclosed. It is also important to make sure you don't end the letter incorrectly.

Sample Task

You see this advertisement in an international student magazine.

Write an application to become a volunteer.

Volunteers needed

We are looking for volunteers to help out at a famous, international sporting event. We're looking for friendly, respectful people with good language skills, good team skills and a 'can-do' attitude. We need people to welcome delegates, provide customer service and solve problems.

If you think you have what it takes, apply now.

- You should write at least 150 words.
- You should spend about 20 minutes on this task.

The first key piece of information in a letter of application is the fact you've seen the advertisement and where you saw it. This will be the perfect way to start the letter.

Remember that you also need to confirm which position it is you're applying for. This exam is designed to be as realistic as possible and in real life there may be more than one position. If you didn't mention the specific job, the reader would obviously not be fully informed.

For example:

Dear Sir or Madam,

I am writing to apply for the Volunteer position advertised in the International Student Magazine.

Language Skills

In this example, the fact that the sporting event international will give you the chance to emphasize your language skills such as your ability to speak English fluently.

As with the letter of reference, language skills are something which you can and should always mention in a letter of application in the IELTS General exam. All positions advertised will require the candidate to speak or write in English.

Suitability for the job

You need to explain your suitability for the job. The question will sometimes state what the required skills or knowledge are, but normally you'll have to include your experience, your qualifications, if any, and personal qualities.

Finally, it would be a good idea to point out that you're available for interview and perhaps to state any times when you're not available. If you cover all these points in your answer clearly, logically, persuasively and in an appropriate format, you should score well in terms of content and communicative achievement.

Sample Response (Letter of Application)

Dear Mr/Mrs/Miss/Ms [Hiring managers name – "Dear Sir or Madam" if name or gender are unknown]

I wish to apply for the role of [Volunteer] advertised in the [International Student Magazine]. Please find enclosed my CV for your consideration.

As you can see from my attached CV, I have over [time period, eg: 5 years] experience in [eg; volunteering or customer service], and I believe the knowledge and skills built up during this time make me the perfect candidate for this position. I am also keen to keep improving my English, as this is not only a hobby but also a real need.

In my current role as a [job title] at [employer name], I have been responsible for [e.g. a 5% increase in revenue], which when coupled with my enthusiasm and dedication [insert skills relevant to the role – usually found in the job description], has helped the business to [measure of success].

I am confident that I can bring this level of success with me to your organisation and help [company name] build upon their reputation as an outstanding company. With my previous experience and expertise, I believe my contribution will have an immediate impact on the business.

Thank you for your time and consideration.

I look forward to meeting with you to discuss my application further.

Yours sincerely/Yours faithfully,

[Your name]

(Word Count 222)

In the next section of this chapter, we look at organizing formal letters and before you move on, if you think you'd benefit from having writing classes with one of our experts, check out our online IELTS Course with one to one Writing classes.

https://www.idmadrid.es/curso-ielts-online-international-english-language-testing-system-online.html

And finally, if you're studying for IELTS on your own and you would like to access our free e-book resources, find out more about our IELTS e-book resources at:

https://www.idmadrid.es/recursos.html

Organisation & Essential Language: Formal Letter of Complaint

As the title suggests, in this section, we are going to focus on features of organization.

In the last section, we looked at two common types of formal letter, which often appear in the exam: the letter of reference and the letter of application. As previously mentioned, both these tasks are very similar in structure and ideas. In this section, we will use a different example, so that you can see the slightly different tone and style required in each type of letter.

Up until now, we have concentrated on spotting the key content. The key content is the information we need to respond to in our letter. If you haven't done this yet, stop for a second and make a note of the key points in the letter of reference and the letter of application.

As we saw in the previous section, we need to respond to all of these key points in our letter if we want to score well in the exam.

Your overall organization of the piece of writing is vital. This includes using logical paragraphs for example, as well as clear organization of ideas within paragraphs. You do this by using linking words, discourse markers and other devices. The examples in the previous section show you exactly how to organize your letter of reference and letter of application but they do not show you how to organize other types of letter.

In this section, we'll look at paragraphing a letter of complaint and also at these additional organizational features.

Read the letter of complaint task below and answer the following question:

Question to think about:

How would you organize the paragraphs in your letter if you were answering this question? Think about how you might organize the underlined points into logical coherent paragraphs.

Formal Letter of Complaint

Task

Read this extract from a letter you have recently sent to a friend:

".... I forgot to say, don't go to Dino's Bar for your birthday. We went there last night - the service was awful, the food was cold and it was so expensive for such a bad meal! I complained to the a member of staff but he asked me to put it in writing ..."

Write your letter of complaint to the manager of Dino´s bar

In your letter:

- Introduce yourself
- Explain the situation
- Say what action you would like the company to take

Write at least 150 words

Question to think about:

How many paragraphs would you have and which power graphs would deal with which issues?

There are several ways to approach this letter, but one suggestion is to organize this around four content paragraphs, one for each problem and one at the end for suggestions.

The answer to this question can be planned and organized as follows:

The letter can be divided into 4 paragraphs:

1. Formal "hello" and state general problem, saying why you went to Dino´s in this case and that you are dissatisfied. State problem 1 (the service was awful)

2. Detailed explanation of problem 2 (the food was cold)

3. Problem 3: the price was expensive

4. Conclusion, what you want Dino´s to do- offer some suggestions here for improvement here.

A bit more on each paragraph:

OK, so the first paragraph is obviously going to deal with your reason for writing. In a letter of complaint, the first main content paragraph is used for outlining the person's problem saying why you went to the business they originally are complaining about and making sure they say that you are dissatisfied.

Then, we could go on to look at the specific details of the problem, using appropriate adjectives.

Finally, in the last paragraph, we could offer some suggestions or recommendations to help the business improve. You can us language such as:

I must insist that you…

I must urge you to…

Essential Language for a Letter of Complaint:

LETTER OF COMPLAINT

I am writing to complain about…

I would like to express my dissatisfaction with …

I am writing to express my concern about the….

I must complain in writing about…

I feel I must complain to you about…

I wish to complain in the strongest terms about…

I am writing to inform you of an apparent error in your records…

Paraphrasing exercise:

Example:

0) Basic Problem: *"I want to complain about the bad service in the restaurant. "*

ii. Key Language: *I would like to express my dissatisfaction with …*

iii, Key Word you must use: POOR (Bad is too informal, so we can use *poor* instead)

iv. Final Product: *"I would like to express my dissatisfaction with the poor standard of service in the restaurant. "*

Now try to complete the process using the following language:

1)

i. Basic problem: *"The cinema is really far away from everything"*

ii. Key Phrase: *I wish to complain in the strongest terms about…*

iii, Key Word: ACCESSIBILITY

iv. Final Product:

....
....
....

2)

i. Basic problem: *"During my course, there were too many students in the class"*

ii. Key Phrase: *I am writing to express my concern about the….*

iii, Key Word: NUMBER

iv. Final Product:

....
....
....

Answers:

1) I wish to complain in the strongest terms about the accessibility of the cinema.

2) I am writing to express my concern about the number of students in the class during my course

Topic specific phrases

- *Poor standard of service/slow service*

- *I am asking for/I would like to request a replacement*

- *No accommodation/Travel delays/Rather rude staff*

- *Badly scratched/dented wrapping/packaging*

- *To claim/demand for a refund*

- *I am returning … to you for correction of the fault/for inspection/repair/servicing*

- *Defective/faulty goods/defective item/machine*

- *The… may need replacing*

- *To restore an item to full working order…*

- *I am enclosing the broken radio in this package; please send me a replacement..*

- *You said that … I feel sure there must be some mistake as I am sure that…*

Ending the letter

- *I do not usually complain, but, as an old customer, I hope you will be interested in my comments.*

- *We look forward to dealing with this matter without delay.*

- *I feel that your company should consider an appropriate refund.*

- *I would be grateful if you would send me a complete refund as soon as possible*

- *We feel there must be some explanation for (this delay) and expect your prompt reply.*

- *Will you please look into this matter and let us know the reason for …*

- *Thank you for your assistance.*

- *I look forward to hearing from you at your earliest convenience.*

- *I am returning the damaged goods/items... and shall be glad if you will replace them.*

- *Please look into this matter at once and let me know the delay.*

- *Please check your records again.*

- *Thank you for your cooperation in correcting this detail...*

- *I wish to draw your attention to...*

- *I would suggest that...*

- *I suggest that immediate steps be taken.*

- *I wish to complain about...*

- *I look forward to a prompt reply and hope that you will take into consideration...*

- *I am really dissatisfied with...*

Now look at the sample answer for the question we looked at earlier in this section. Pay special attention to the language and structure used.

<u>**Sample Answer**</u>

Dear Sir/Madam,

I would like to express my dissatisfaction with the poor standard of service we received during our recent visit to Dino´s Bar. Firstly, the staff were generally quite rude and unhelpful, they seemed to lack basic food knowledge and they did not seem interested in the job. For instance, none of them could offer any advice to me on choosing a dish.

A further cause for complaint was that the food was cold when it arrived to our table. I understand that it was a busy night, but, we booked the table and the menus the day before, so I feel that they should have been ready.

Finally, not only did we receive substandard food and unfriendly, unhelpful service, but we were also charged full price for our meals after we complained. In my opinion the prices seem to be very expensive for the quality of the food and the service provided.

I do not usually complain, but, as a loyal customer, I hope you will be interested in my comments. Perhaps it would be appropriate to offer some training courses to staff at Dino´s Bar, in order to avoid this from happening again. I feel that customer service was a big issue, as was the quality of the food. If these two problems were fixed, then price might not be such an issue in the future, as customers would be happy to pay little more for a better experience. I hope you will take these points into consideration

I look forward to your reply.

Yours faithfully,

Name and Surname

Formal Letters: Structure Rules

Greeting

Name unknown: *Dear Sir/Madam,*

Name known: *Dear Mr.../ Dear Mrs... / Dear Ms.. + surname*

Reason for writing

I am writing to ... I am writing with regard to ...

I am writing on behalf of ...

Asking questions

I would be grateful if ...   I wonder if you could ....

Could you ...?

Referring to someone else´s letter /points

As you stated in your letter, ... Regarding .../ Concerning ...

With regard to ....

Finishing the letter

If you require any further information, please do not hesitate to contact me.

I look forward to hearing from you.

Signing

If Dear + name = Yours sincerely,

If Dear Sir/ Madam = Yours faithfully

Your first name + surname must be written clearly under your signature

Formal Letter IELTS General Exam Checklist.

When you have written your letter, check:

1. It is a formal letter

2. It includes all the information necessary

3. You have asked all the questions you need to

4. The questions are correctly formulated indirect questions

5. The letter is divided into paragraphs

6. You have checked the letter carefully for mistakes

Formal Letters: Language

Letters can be anything from very formal to very informal. The IELTS General Writing paper will never ask you to write a specialized business or legal letter requiring a professional knowledge of business words, structures and expressions. However, they might ask you to write a formal, a semi-formal or an informal email or letter.

In this section of the chapter, we will focus on your use of language and in particular, your ability to create a formal register. This will help you to do well in two of the assessment criteria: language of course in terms of using a range of formal vocabulary and grammatical structures and communicative achievement by being able to create an appropriate formal tone that has a positive effect on the reader. We will identify some of the features of formal English that we often find in formal letters.

At the end of this section you will find a list of useful formal-informal equivalents. This list will save you a lot of time in your preparation for the exam. For example, in a letter of complaint: *"I was rather disappointed"* is a formal way of saying *"I was furious"* or *"I was very angry"*. See how many more formal and informal equivalent items you can learn next.

Exercise 1:

Transform the informal or semi-formal version of each phrase from a letter of complaint into a formal style. You can make small changes to the content of the sentences if you think it's necessary and you can use a dictionary.

Example: I thought I'd write = I am writing

a. state of the playground =

....

b. I have noticed loads of rubbish =

....

c. I reckon =

....

d. The teacher I'm talking about =

....

e. On top of this =

....

f. a load of problems =

....

g. You could =

....

h. stop =

....

i. What's more =

....

j. better =

....

k. To finish =

....

l. I´m looking forward to hearing from you =

....

Answers:

a. state of the playground = condition of the playground

b. I have noticed loads of rubbish = There is a great deal of litter

c. I reckon = It is my opinion that…

d. The teacher I'm talking about = The teacher in question OR The teacher I am referring to

e. On top of this = Furthermore

f. a load of problems = a number of problems

g. You could = it may be possible for you

h. stop = prevent

i. What's more = In addition

j. better = more suitable OR more adequate

k. To finish = In conclusion

l. I'm looking forward to hearing from you = I look forward to your reply OR I look forward to hearing from you

Exercise 2:

Now here are some full sentences from formal letters. Complete the sentences using only one word.

a. I am writing in .... to your job advertisement in the ABC newspaper

b. I would like to .... for the position of translator.

c. I am .... to come for interview at any time convenient to you.

d. I would be .... if you could send me further information regarding the position.

e. Please find my CV ....

f. I would like to express my .... with the poor standard of service we received during our recent visit to your cinema.

g. For ...., none of them could offer any advice to me on choosing a dish.

h. Finally, not only .... we receive substandard food and unfriendly, unhelpful service, but we were also charged full price for our meals after we complained.

i. I look forward to your reply.

Answers:

a. I am writing in reply/ response to your job advertisement in the ABC newspaper

b. I would like to apply for the position of translator.

c. I am available/ able to come for interview at any time convenient to you.

d. I would be grateful if you could send me further information regarding the position.

e. Please find my CV attached (email)/ enclosed (letter).

f. I would like to express my dissatisfaction with the poor standard of service we received during our recent visit to your cinema.

g. For instance, none of them could offer any advice to me on choosing a dish.

h. Finally, not only did we receive substandard food and unfriendly, unhelpful service, but we were also charged full price for our meals after we complained.

i. I look forward to your reply.

Use of the Passive (Sometimes)

Okay, the next example is one where the passive has been used instead of an active form. This is a common feature of formal writing but should not be overused.

This sentence is an example of how we might structure a sentence formally.

Informal: *"The waiter did offer us another dish, but when it arrived it was cold again."*

Formal: *"Although we were offered an alternative dish, when it was delivered to the table it was cold again".*

Notice two clauses in the informal version are joined by but whereas in the formal version, the two clauses have been reversed and but is replaced with although which starts the sentence. This is a more formal way of saying the same thing.

Within the formal sentence *"Although we were offered an alternative dish, when it was delivered to the table it was cold again",* there are further examples of vocabulary that is more formal than the equivalent in the informal version. For example, *alternative dish* is a more formal way of saying *another dish*.

As we saw above, phrasal verbs are most typical of informal letters — although there are some which have no more formal equivalents and are common in all types of letter (*look forward to,* for example). Most phrasal verbs, however, do have formal equivalents and these would be preferred in most formal letters whereas the formal equivalents would be very rarely used in an informal letter.

6 Quick Rules of Formal VS Informal:

1. We tend to understate our feelings and would say *I was rather disappointed* or *I was somewhat surprised* instead of saying how we really felt.

2. For the same reason, we do not use exclamation marks.

3. We often use the passive to emphasize the action when the person is of less importance

4. We avoid contractions in formal letters.

5. We use formal equivalence of idiomatic language and phrasal verbs

6. Particular sentence structures can be used to create a formal tone. Inversion is one example of this "Although we were offered an alternative dish, when it was delivered to the table it was cold again".

Exercise 3:

Rewrite the following sentences using formal equivalents for the phrasal verbs. Use a dictionary if necessary. You might need to make other changes to the structures.

1) I'm so chuffed that you've been talked into coming to the meeting.

....
..

....
..

2) The football club's facilities have been done up, so this should make our performances better.

....
..

....
..

3) As our town is quite cut off, perhaps we could arrange for you to be put up in a hotel in the city for a few days.

....
..

....
..

4) We will make up for the inconvenience of having to wait for so long.

....
..

....
..

Answers:

1) I am very happy that you have been convinced to attend the meeting.

2) The football club's facilities have been refurbished, which should improve our performances.

3) As our town is quite isolated, we could arrange hotel accommodation in the city for a few days.

4) We will compensate you for the inconvenience of having to wait for so long.

Chapter 2:

Informal Letters

The informal letter is going to be very friendly, very relaxed, very easy language.

LET'S START WITH A TYPICAL TASK.

An English-speaking friend is visiting your region for a couple of weeks during his holidays and has written to you to ask for several recommendations.

Write a letter to your friend.

In your letter you should:

• offer to help find accommodation

• give advice about things to do

• provide information about what clothes to bring..

In this type of task, you should begin your letter as follows:

Dear … your friend's name.

A few things to keep in mind.

• You have about 20 minutes to write this.

• You should have at least 150 words. Aim for about 180 (a little bit more but don't go too long- If you're over 240 words, you've written much more than you need to.)

• Address the points, have your opening and closing and that's it!

Let's start with the general idea of what you're trying to do, what you're trying to accomplish.

The tone:

'The tone' of the letter means how your letter sounds, or the overall feeling it gives the reader. It should be very relaxed, very informal, this is what the examiners are looking for.

For example: if you're writing to your friend, write it as though you were speaking to your friend; very casual.

You can start with:

Dear- Hello- Hi and then the person´s first name, never their surname.

You shouldn´t use *Mr., Mrs., Dr.*.

Do not put first and last name because you do not address your friend or family member by his or her first and last name in real life.

Use contractions:

Now contractions are suitable. So in terms of how you're going to use I've, it's, don't etc.., In a formal letter, you say do not whereas in an informal letter, you say don't.

Slang and idioms

Not only are slang and idioms okay now, they're actually recommended because they demonstrate that you can adapt your language to different contexts. When you speak with your friends, you normally use very casual language including slang and idioms.

Nevertheless, remember it has to be natural, so don't be too heavy on the slang or the idioms. One or two here and there are great, but if you overuse them, it becomes unnatural and the examiners may penalise you for it.

Note that you can use idioms in your formal letter as well but very carefully, very selectively and it has to be very appropriate, so it´s generally not recommended.

Stay organized and focused:

You still have to remember what it is you're doing and make it very clear in the letter. Are you thanking the person, are you answering a question, are you asking for something, are you offering advice? Make this clear right away in the introduction. Make sure the body follows.

Language

Again, you don't want to use very serious language in an informal letter or email, you don't want to use too many formal or complex words because that's not how we speak to friends and family normally.

With our friends we're usually very casual and relaxed.

For example:

I just wanted to say thanks for helping me out last week.

In a formal letter, you would write

I'm writing to express my appreciation and gratitude for your assistance with last week's matter..

Notice the different feel of the two sentences. One is very casual, one is very formal.

Another example:

Should you require any further information, please do not hesitate to contact me - formal.

Versus

Let me know if you need anything else - super casual.

To make your letter look real, the best thing you can do is ALWAYS rely on your personal experience.

Formal VS Informal Language List:

It is vital that you can distinguish between formal and informal language in English, not only for this exam, but also for communication in general. Writing a letter or email to a friend is obviously not the same as writing a letter of recommendation for a friend who has applied for a job. Here are some examples of formal and informal words with the same meaning,

VERBS:

FORMAL: INFORMAL

to depart: to go

to carry out: to do

to provide: to give

to retain: keep

to cease: stop

to seek: look for

assist, aid: to help

liberate: to free

obtain: to get

to desire: want

request: to ask for

to function: work

to demonstrate: show

to reside: live

require: need

OTHER WORDS:

FORMAL: INFORMAL

subsequently: next / later

immature, infantile: childish

sufficient: enough

further: more (information)

hence, therefore: so

deficiency, lack of: little, there is no

perspiration: sweat

inexpensive: cheap

☐

Chapter 3:

IELTS Essay

IELTS Writing Task 2 Marking Scheme

What IELTS examiners look for in IELTS Task 1 and Task 2

Task achievement	Did you understand and answer the question? Is there a clear opinion? What information did you include? Are there at least 250 words?
Organization	How well did you plan and organize the writing task? Did you use good connecting words?
Vocabulary	What vocabulary did you use? Did you use it well? How good is the spelling? To get a high band score you must: • Have a good range of vocabulary used correctly. • Attempts to use less common vocabulary and uses it correctly a lot of the time. • Very few or no spelling mistakes
Grammar	What grammar did you use? Did you use it well? How good is the punctuation? To get a high band score you must: • Produce a lot of error-free sentences. • Use a variety of complex sentences and have good

| | control of grammar |
| | • Have good control of punctuation |

Task 2 in the IELTS writing exam is essential if you want to get a high band score in the exam. It is surprisingly easy to improve your writing score considerably as long as you are prepared to take some advice and practise, practise, practise.

The most common IELTS Writing Task 2 structures are:

Opinion Essay

Example:

Space exploration is much too expensive and the money should be spent on more important things.

What is your opinion?

Advantages and Disadvantages Essay

Some people believe that it is better to take a gap year before going to university, while others think that this can be a waste of time and that going straight into higher education is the best option.

Discuss both views and give your opinion.

Problem Essay

Despite a large number of gyms, a sedentary lifestyle is gaining popularity in the contemporary world.

What problems are associated with this?

What solutions can you suggest?

Opinion Essay

Focus on the topic and the task

Opinion essay instructions have two parts. You must understand both the topic and the task before you start the essay.

The first part tells you the topic of the essay:

Some people think that more money should be invested into space exploration as it is a vital form of investigation for the future of humanity, while others believe it is a waste of vital funding which could otherwise be used towards more important projects here on earth.

The second part of the question gives you the specific task you must complete to get marks:

Discuss both these views and give your own opinion.

Understanding the topic of the essay

There are normally three ways the opinion essay can be presented in the exam:

Type 1: Two **opposite views** to discuss:

"Some people think that more money should be invested into space exploration as it is a vital form of investigation for the future of humanity, while others believe it is a waste of vital funding which could otherwise be used towards more important projects here on earth. "

Type 2: "Two **opposite views** to discuss using the word *should* in the instruction.

Should more money be invested into space exploration or should it be used towards more important projects here on earth? "

Type 3: A **statement** to discuss:

"Paying for space exploration is a waste of vital funding which could otherwise be used towards more important projects here on earth. "

Connecting words and set phrases

Putting your reasons in order	Firstly/Secondly. Thirdly/Finally
Expressing an opinion	I hold the view that ... In my view... It is probably true to say that.... There can be no doubt that ...
Mentioning what other people think	It has been suggested that.... There are those who believe that.. There are those who argue that... Opponents/ supporters of (e.g. hunting) ... argue that.... Most people hold firmly to the belief that... It is often claimed that...
Common opinions in society	It is widely believed/thought that Few people would contest that.... Nobody would dispute the fact that .... It is generally agreed that...
Referring to evidence and facts	Research suggests that... All the evidence suggests that ... Recent evidence indicates that .....
Changing direction	However/Nevertheless
Giving examples	For example for instance such as
Concluding	In conclusion / Overall,

Chapter 4:

Writing Like A Pro: How To Write Advanced English Without Writing "Advanced" English

The IELTS essay in Task 2 of the IELTS writing exam is something that many students get nervous about. <u>Many students overcomplicate their lives by trying to express simple ideas in a complex way</u>. The result is a collection of illogical and unnatural sentences which have very little meaning, and which the examiner struggles to understand. This is the perfect recipe for failure in the exam.

"The definition of genius is taking the complex and making it simple."

— Albert Einstein

"Simplicity is the glory of expression."

— Walt Whitman

The biggest problem when it comes to improving your writing are your ideas of what good writing in English, or in any language actually is. Try to think of a **definition of 'good writing'** for a second...

A definition from The Harvard University Writing Centre:

Writing a good academic essay means presenting a logical set of ideas to create an argument or opinion. Essays are linear—they offer one idea at a time—they must present their ideas in the order that makes most sense to a reader. Successfully structuring an essay means presenting the ideas in a logical way to the reader.

2000, Elizabeth Abrams, for the Writing Center at Harvard University

You will notice how it doesn't say anywhere in the definition that a good essay uses complicated language or prioritises complex sentences over logical sentences. It's all about logic, the complex language will come, but it must come naturally, appropriately, and more importantly from logical thinking.

The trick to improving your writing is to keep it simple! When you over-think what you are writing and build structures thinking only about making them complex, that is when grammar problems happen and essay disasters occur! Think of each sentence you write as a small house: you have to start with a simple, solid and clear base. Then you can decorate it to make it sound "Advanced" and professional, but the initial base has to be made of a solid idea or group of ideas expressed in a clear and direct way.

Don´t forget the basic grammar rules of English. These rules do not change just because you are writing an essay!

Note: It is important to give your opinion clearly.

Exercise 1:

Essay structures: Writing "Advanced" English

As already mentioned, writing advanced English is not as hard as it may initially seem.

Try the following exercise to help you improve your writing:

The original sentences are too personal, too informal and sound too simple for an essay. Use the key phrase in CAPITALS to complete the second sentence so that it means the same as the first sentence. Try to completely change the original sentence while retaining the same basic message.

1. Vegetables are good for you but meat is also good for you.

NOBODY WOULD DISPUTE THE FACT THAT...

. . . .
. . . .
. . . .

2. Newspapers lie.

IT IS PROBABLY TRUE TO SAY THAT.....

. . . .
. . . .
. . . .

3. Lots of people like chocolate because it is delicious, but it makes people fat.

FEW PEOPLE WOULD CONTEST THAT....

....

....

....

And now a particularly challenging sentence... Tips: Remember words like hence, therefore, as a result, in turn etc...

4. If people have jobs they have more money so they buy more things. When people buy more things, businesses sell more things. This is good for businesses. When businesses sell more things they need more people. When businesses need more people they employ them, so more people get jobs and have money to spend. It´s a circle of capitalist awesomeness.

ALL THE EVIDENCE SUGGESTS THAT......

....

....

....

Suggested Answers:

1. **Nobody would dispute the fact that** vegetables have a positive impact on health, **however** meat is also vital **in order to** maintain a healthy and balanced lifestyle.

2. **It is probably true to say that** newspapers and other media often distort the truth.

3. **Few people would contest that** chocolate is very popular due to its taste, however it can often lead to obesity and other health issues.

4. **All the evidence suggests that** an increase in the level of employment would lead to higher levels of spending (which would benefit businesses) and **in turn** increase employment further as businesses would seek to meet the increase in demand.

OR

All the evidence suggests that an increase in the level of employment would lead to higher levels of spending (which would benefit businesses). This, **in turn**, would increase employment (further) as businesses would seek to meet the increase in demand.

Exercise 2

Fill the gaps with an appropriate word or phrase from the box:

To conclude	I hold the view that	however.	Firstly, research suggests that
may	which can lead to	For instance,	when people
they are more likely to	Secondly, few people would contest that	Therefore	it is likely that
Finally,	such as	However, there are those who argue that	nobody would contest the fact that
In addition, it is often claimed that	Nobody would dispute the fact that	there can be no doubt that	Hence,

Model Essay

.... many programs on television include violent scenes, especially action and horror movies. .... they should not be allowed, ... many people disagree with this opinion. In this essay, I will discuss both sides and give reasons for my opinion.

.........., ... people who watch violent programs and play violent computer games .... worry more about their own safety, ... problems in society. ...., ... are worried about their safety, ... react aggressively towards strangers. .... some children copy what they see on television and in computer games. ...... if they are watching and interacting with violence on a daily basis .... they will copy this type of behavior. ...., there are more beneficial activities that children could be participating in, ... playing a sport or reading a book.

.... violence is not something we learn from television and computer games. For example, ... there were murders before television and videogames were invented. ...., ... children cannot watch violent programs and play inappropriate videogames easily. For instance, there are restrictions for some programmes and games, and many parents do not allow their children to watch television after a certain time.

................, although there are some reasonable arguments against higher restrictions on violent videogames and programmes for children, ... the potential disadvantages of children copying what they see and hear in these programmes and games far outweigh the advantages of having free access to them. Furthermore, current restrictions are ineffective and easy to ignore. ...., governments and local institutions should do more to promote alternative activities and to engage young people in their local communities from an early age.

Answers:

Nobody would dispute the fact that many programs on television include violent scenes, especially action and horror movies. **I hold the view that** they should not be allowed, **however** many people disagree with this opinion. In this essay, I will discuss both sides and give reasons for my opinion.

Firstly, **research suggests that** people who watch violent programs and play violent computer games **may** worry more about their own safety, **which can lead to** problems in society. **For instance**, **when people** are worried about their safety, **they are more likely to** react aggressively towards strangers. **Secondly**, **few people would contest that** some children copy what they see on television and in computer games. **Hence**, if they are watching and interacting with violence on a daily basis **it is likely that** they will copy this type of behavior. **Finally**, there are more beneficial activities that children could be participating in **such as** playing a sport or reading a book.

However, there are those who argue that violence is not something we learn from television and computer games. For example, **nobody would contest the fact that** there were murders before television and videogames were invented. **In addition**, **it is often claimed that** children cannot watch violent programs and play inappropriate videogames easily. For instance, there are restrictions for some programmes and games, and many parents do not allow their children to watch television after a certain time.

To conclude, although there are some reasonable arguments against higher restrictions on violent videogames and programmes for children, **there can be no doubt that** the potential disadvantages of children copying what they see and hear in these programmes and games far outweigh the advantages of having free access to them. Furthermore, current restrictions are ineffective and easy to ignore. **Therefore**, governments and local institutions should do more to promote alternative activities and to engage young people in their local communities from an early age.

The Structure of Paragraphs

A paragraph normally has three parts:

1. a sentence that introduces the topic or gist of the paragraph (and **can** link it to the previous paragraph)

2. 2-3 sentences that develop the topic (with analysis, evidence or detail)

3. 1 sentence that concludes the topic (or links it to the next paragraph).- This is optional in the IELTS essay

Have a look at some example paragraphs, where each section has been numbered 1-3.

(1) There is no doubt that corruption is the most important point to focus on, because it originates from positions of power. **(2)** Corruption can take many shapes and forms, such as political, which involves crimes in a country's legal system and within the police, and economic, for example by misusing tax money. **(3)** All the evidence suggests that countries with corrupt governments are not able to develop as fast as countries where there is less corruption.

(1) Another obstacle which developing countries face nowadays is the loss of investments. **(2)** When there is a fast movement of investments out of a country it can cause problems. This situation can happen as a result of economic reasons, such as an increase in taxes, or it can happen due to political problems, such as wars or corruption. **(3)** These issues can have an extremely negative effect on the level of trust that people have in their governments, and investors may choose to invest in other countries.

Vocabulary Boost:
Obstacle (obstacles)- **Countable Noun**
Refer to anything that makes it difficult for you to do something as an obstacle.

Connecting Paragraphs to each other

When you start a new paragraph, you are telling the reader that the previous point is finished and you are starting something new. Nevertheless, this new paragraph is not disconnected from the previous one, and you need to communicate to the reader what the connection is. For instance, if you start with *However, there are those who argue that violence is not something we learn from television and computer games...* then the structure you have used signals to the reader that you are discussing a different argument ('However,') which contradicts the previous ideas ('However') and which is expressed by other people not you 'there are those who argue that'. You have communicated a lot of information to the reader with only seven words (*However, there are those who argue that...*). This is one of the definitions of good writing- effective while using as few words as possible to maintain clarity.

"Another argument is that…"

If you start a new paragraph with the phrase 'Another argument in favour of stricter laws is that crime is directly related to…' then you are signaling to the reader that you are changing to a different argument ('Another') with the same purpose ('in favour of..').

To give more specific information use 'This argument …'.

This is a handy structure to learn and which can be adapted to many different contexts.

The words in the box below are all useful examples of words like 'argument', which you can use with the word 'this' (or 'these' in plural) to specify more information.

analysis	approach	concept	context
data	definition	environment	evidence
factor	function	interpretation	issue
measure	method	period	policy
principle	procedure	process	research
response	sector	structure	Theory

Here is an example of how we can use this structure in an essay.

There is no doubt that corruption is the most important point to focus on, because it originates from positions of power. Corruption can take many shapes and forms, such as political, which involves crimes in a country's legal system and within the police, and economic, for example by misusing tax money. All the evidence suggests that countries with corrupt governments are not able to develop as fast as countries where there is less corruption.

These factors […].

OR

This negative environment […].

The first sentence of a paragraph is vital, as it shows how it connects with the overall structure, and can signal what will happen next.

When you practice writing, always check that your essay is logical by underlining the most important sentences in each paragraph. You should be able to understand the whole essay only by reading those sentences. If you can't, you need to make changes.

The beginning of the essay

To get the highest grades in the IELTS exam the essay has to introduce the topic, so you must begin with a relatively general statement. However, the trick is not to over-generalize, otherwise the statement becomes meaningless and can be annoying to read. For example, the following first sentence of an essay is too vague or general and the structure which is used is not appropriate.

First sentence of essay

There are those who argue that water is necessary for human life and therefore water shortage is one of the most important problems in the world.

Comments

Water is vital to human life and this is an absolute fact, not something that people can argue about. The student wanted to use *'There are those who argue that'*, but this structure is wrong for the meaning of the sentence. The statement is also too general and it is not clear what this essay is about.

Possible improvement

Water shortages affect millions of people worldwide each year, and there is evidence which suggests that they are becoming increasingly difficult to tackle due to climate change.

You will see in the comments section above that it is a bad idea to memorize words or structures ('There are those who argue that', 'nobody would dispute the fact that...' etc..) to insert your ideas into. As we discussed in previous chapters, each sentence and paragraph are like a house which need logical, solid foundations before you decorate them. It is better to start with your ideas and then to think about how you can express them best.

Expressing the importance of the topic

Superlatives can be useful to indicate that the topic is important:

		causes of ...	is ...
(one of) **the most**	significant important	problems of ...	

| (some of) **the most** | | conditions for ... | are ... |
| | | aspects of ... | |

... is	(one of) **the most**	significant important	causes of ... problems of ... conditions for ... aspects of ...

The following **adjective** and noun combinations can also be useful:

Adjective - Noun combinations

increasing concern	an **important** part	a **key** role/factor	a **great/major** problem
a **central** area of	a **common** problem	an **increasing** need/concern	**heightened** awareness
rapid development	a **dramatic** increase	**renewed/unprecedented** interest	a **serious** effect/impact on

You can also use the following combinations with **adverbs**:

is becoming **increasingly** important	is becoming **increasingly** challenging	has been **extensively** researched

Efficiency

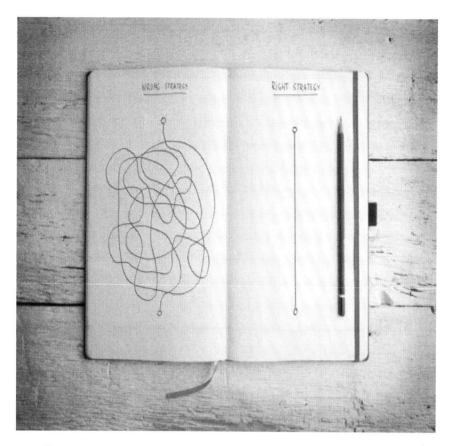

Efficient writing expresses an idea, opinion, reason or consequence without using too many words. A big mistake many students make is that they try to fill the page with words thinking this will make them finish the essay sooner and that it will look good because it means they know a lot. This is completely wrong for most if not all exams, whether it's the IELTS or a university exam. Always use the minimum number of words possible and do not repeat yourself.

According to Google, the definition of efficiency is: "maximum productivity with minimum wasted effort or expense". In your writing, this means few words but lots of meaning. **Note:** remember that in the IELTS, the word count indicated in the exam is a minimum not a maximum, so you still need to reach this minimum or you will be penalised but you should avoid repetition and meaningless sentences by carefully proofreading your writing before you finish.

Using nouns in writing

If you pay attention to the best essay examples and the best writing in general, you will notice that many noun phrases are used. Here is an example:

"At an investigative level the availability of digital resources, simulators and other tools provide the researcher with increased access to information, which otherwise would not be accessible. "

A large portion of that sentence is made up of nouns. Using nouns is extremely efficient, whereas using verbs can be long and repetitive in an essay or description at times.

For example, you use less space if you are talking about processes without describing the action:

Temperature increase	they have increased the temperature
efficiency increase (increase in efficiency)	They have increased the efficiency

Note: Ideally, you should aim to have a mixture of structures to avoid repetition.

Exercise 2

Change the sentences by using nouns instead of verbs where possible.

The trick is to find the verbs first, then transform some of them into nouns, e.g.:

The area would benefit if businesses increased the amount they produced.

The area would benefit from an increase in business productivity/business production.

1. The local government should train their employees better so that they can be more efficient.

....

....

....
....

2. There is a difference between cultures so they need to communicate by using different strategies.

....
....

....
....

3. If governments around the world implement this strategy, they may reduce the pollution.

....
....

....
....

4. If they recycle waste, they may have a better chance of reducing poverty in the area

....
....

....
....

Exercise 2

Suggested Answers

1. *Better employee training would increase the local government's efficiency. / With better employee training the local government's efficiency would increase.*

2. *Cultural differences need/require a wide range of/different communication strategies.*

3. *The implementation of this strategy by (world) governments may lead to reductions in pollution.*

4. *The recycling of waste may improve chances of reducing poverty in the area / may lead to a reduction of poverty in the area / may lead to an improved chance of reducing poverty in the area.*

The IELTS General writing exam prepares you for writing within an academic and professional setting where you need to be respectful of the ideas of others. In your essays it would look very bad if you said something like 'These people are completely wrong' or 'I think these researchers were wrong'. Instead, you would need to express yourself in a more diplomatic way, for example: 'However, it might be the case that ....' or 'Recent research suggests that this is not the case.' You are supposed to analyse different sides and project a sense of impartiality while you say whether you agree or disagree. Remember you always need to remain modest about your opinion and show the reader that you understand that you may be wrong just like anybody else.

<u>Here are some examples:</u>

"Students have a very low level of basic mathematical knowledge due to over-dependence on calculators."

This is the student's personal opinion, but she/he cannot write this without evidence. In the IELTS exam you are not likely going to be able to cite real evidence to support your arguments, so you need to change your language: "Over-dependence on calculators **may** have a negative effect on the basic mathematical knowledge of **some students**"

Use cautious language. This is also called 'hedging' language, because 'to hedge against something' means to protect yourself from its negative consequences.

Students often make the mistake using cautious language where it is not appropriate. They sometimes use 'would', 'might', 'likely to', etc. because they have learnt that these verbs are common in English writing.

For example: "Annual financial reports **<u>might</u> include information from financial statements and other sources.***"*

You don't need to know a lot about accounting or business to know that the objective of financial reports is to provide financial information taken from financial statements and other sources. Therefore, the verb 'might' can't be used here.

Vocabulary: Being Specific enough

Exercise 3

Eliminate the word 'thing' in these sentences and add a more specific word or phrase.

1. The availability of water has a significant effect on every living thing.

2. This environment is made up of non-living things like air, water and rocks.

3. It is essential from a scientific perspective to investigate every single thing that is possible.

Exercise 3:

Suggested Answers:

1. *The availability of water has a significant effect on every living* **organism/being**.

2. *This environment is made up of non-living* **elements** *like air, water and rocks.*

3. *It is essential from a scientific perspective to investigate every single* **possibility/possible factor**.

Remember...

Link your sentences in IELTS Writing

Always use Linking Adverbs like therefore, additionally, consequently, firstly, secondly, finally, moreover, however

Use synonyms to replace basic level vocabulary

To (purpose): in order to, so as to

Like = such as, for example, for instance

Get = receive, acquire, obtain

Help = aid, assist, support

Not only does X do Y but it also does Z

Look at the difference between these sentences....

Version 1: Working gives you experience to help your career. Working also improves important skills like social skills.

Version 2: Not only does working provide you with experience to assist your career, but it also improves essential skills such as social abilities and communication.

Chapter 5: Useful Language

The IELTS Writing Checklist

PREPARATIONS

- Look through your written work and check what mistakes you made

- Do any exercises/past papers that have not been done yet.

- Time yourself for reading and writing!!!

- Have a look at the list of phrases for *Writing 1 and 2* and highlight the ones that you use the most often.

- Read all Model and Authentic Answers for *Writing 1 and 2,* underline all the important phrases used.

  - Read the section ***Things to Remember*** below

CHECKLIST - THE DAY BEFORE THE EXAM:

- Write down a few phrases that you use the most often in your written assignments and that you would like to use in exam in *Writing*

- *task 1 and 2;*

- Check if you have your passport (or any other proof of identity)

- ready for the exam;

- Write down a few phrases that you are going to use in your presentation about yourself for *Speaking part 1;*

- Have a relaxing evening and don't worry!

- I am sure you will do the best you can!

I' m keeping my fingers crossed for you!

THINGS TO REMEMBER

WRITING: TASK 1

Expressing figures and quantities

- Take time to read and understand the title of the question.

- Check you understand the type of writing you need to do.

- Be careful to express yourself correctly.

- Use a variety of structures

The opening statement

- Don't copy text from the question.

- Stick to the information they ask for.

- Specific details are not needed in the opening section.

TASK 2

Understanding the topic and the task

- Make sure you understand what the topic or subject of questions is. Underline the key words if necessary.

- Read the questions carefully to identify exactly what you need to.

- Focus on the question itself, not on what you want to write about.

Brainstorming and planning

- You must write at least number of words specified or you will lose marks.

- You will not have time to count words in the exam, so count words when you are practising so you know roughly how to write.

- It is important to generate ideas as quickly as possible.

- Use mindmaps, spidegrams and list to organise information quickly.

- A good essay or composition must have a beginning, middle and an end.

- Decide what you are going to write and make a brief plan outlining what each paragraphs will contain.

- Write brief notes on what on what you want to include in each paragraph. This helps to prompt you as you write your essay and serves as a useful checklist when you have finished.

- A useful guiding to follow is to write an introduction of approximately 50 words, the main body of 170 words or more and a conclusion of 30-40 words. However, these amounts are flexible.

THE INTRODUCTION

Aim and contents

- Don't copy out the question. You will not gain marks for this.

- The introduction needs to be relevant to the question.

- Write in an impersonal, formal style.

THE MAIN BODY

Aim and contents

- Paragraphs and topics sentences give your writing structure and provide links between sections.

- Use linking words to give your writing cohesion.

CONCLUSION

Aim and contents

- The conclusion must refer back to the points made in the essay. Don't include new information.

- The conclusion can sum up you views but for best marks should be written in an impersonal, formal style.

Useful Language

IELTS- WRITING TASK 1

Formal VS Informal Language List:

It is vital that you can distinguish between formal and informal language in English, not only for this exam, but also for communication in general. Writing a letter or email to a friend is obviously not the same as writing a letter of recommendation for a friend who has applied for a job. Here are some examples of formal and informal words with the same meaning,

VERBS:

FORMAL: INFORMAL

to depart: to go

to carry out: to do

to provide: to give

to retain: keep

to cease: stop

to seek: look for

assist, aid: to help

liberate: to free

obtain: to get

to desire: want

request: to ask for

to function: work

to demonstrate: show

to reside: live

require: need

OTHER WORDS:

FORMAL: INFORMAL

subsequently: next / later

immature, infantile: childish

sufficient: enough

further: more (information)

hence, therefore: so

deficiency, lack of: little, there is no

perspiration: sweat

inexpensive: cheap

IELTS- WRITING - TASK 2

USEFUL PHRASES

- If you consider... you could be convinced by an argument in favour of....
- But you have to think about another aspect of the problem...
- I do not feel this is a direct cause of...
- Of course it goes without saying that...
- There has been a growing body of opinion that..
- ... the situation can be addressed by adopting the methods mentioned above...
- While I admit that... I would argue that...
- One approach would be...
- A second possibility would be to...
- Obviously,...
- However,
- This suggests that...
- In addition...
- To sum up...
- In fact..
- I tend to disagree...
- I am unconvinced by...
- Overall,...
- In the final analysis...
- Ultimately,...
- To conclude...
- In conclusion...
- On the other hand...

- There is no doubt that…
- This could involve…
- Thirdly…

EXPRESSING VIEWS

- I would argue that…
- I firmly believe that…
- It seems to me that..
- I tend to think that…
- People argue that..
- Some people think that…
- Many people feel that…
- In my experience…
- It is undoubtedly true that..
- It is certainly true that….

REFUTING AN ARGUMENT

- I am unconvinced that…
- I don not believe that..
- It I hard to accept that…
- It is unjustifiable to say that…
- There is little evidence to support that…

PROVIDING SUPPORT

- For example,…
- For instance,…

- Indeed,…
- In fact,…
- Of course,…
- It can be generally observed that…
- Statistics demonstrate…
- If this is/were the case…
- Firstly,…
- Naturally,…
- In my experience…
- Let me illustrate…

DEFINING/EXPLAINING

- I would argue that…
- By this I mean…
- In other words..
- This is to say…
- To be more precise..
- Here I am referring to …

USE SPARINGLY (=a little)

- First/second, etc…
- Moreover..
- In addition…
- Furthermore,…
- Nevertheless/nonetheless…
- On the one/other hand…
- Besides…

- Consequently…
- In contrast…
- In comparison…

USE MODERATELY

- While…
- Meanwhile…
- Although…
- In spite of…/ Despite the fact that…
- Even though…
- As a result…
- However…
- Since…
- Similarly…
- Thus…
- In turn

OTHER USEFUL PHRASES

- My response to this argument depend on what is meant by…
- There is surely a difference between…. and….
- I intend to illustrate how some of these differences are significant to the argument put forward.
- However, whilst I agree that… I am less convinced that…
- I certainly believe that…
- One of the main arguments in favour of…. is that…
- In other words…
- Admittedly, in some ways…

- Surely…
- Arguably..
- Either way…
- In any case…
- The most important point is that…
- Another point is that…
- Of crucial importance , in my opinion, is…
- There is , however, another possible way of defining…
- …that I am in favour of , although I also realise that…
- Therefore…
- There is no doubt that…
- However, it is possible to tackle this serious issue in a number of ways.
- One approach would be..
- …would be particularly beneficial.
- A second possibility would be to…
- …this could involve…
- Many people feel that this is unacceptable because…
- Opponents of… point out that … and argue that…
- On the other hand it cannot be denied that…
- Supporters of…argue that…

INTRODUCING A FALSE ARGUMENT

- *It could be argued that…*
- *Some people would argue that…*
- *There is also the idea implicit in the statement that…*
- *It is often suggested that…*

DEMOLISHING A FALSE ARGUMENT

- *This is partly true, but…*
- *To a certain limited extant, there is some truth in this…*
- *However, the implication that… is oversimplification.*
- *This argument has certain specific logic, but…*

PROPOSING A CORRECT ARGUMENT

- *It is clear that…*
- *The real situation…*
- *Obviously…*
- *On the contrary…*
- *It is therefore quite wrong to suggest that…*

<u>REMEMBER! AN ESSAY CONTAINS:</u>

INTRO

- ✓ *About 50 words*
- ✓ *General statement about the topic*
- ✓ *The purpose of the essay*
- ✓ *Initial views of the writer on the subject*

BODY

- ✓ *About 170 words*
- ✓ *Develops the key ideas and topic mentioned in the intro*
- ✓ *consist of 2-3 paragraphs*
- ✓ *related to the opening and closing paragraphs*

CONCLUSION

- ✓ 30-40 words
- ✓ No new info!
- ✓ sums up the key points covered in the essay

REMEMBER!

- Read the questions very carefully.

- Underline key points in the question and make sure is relevant to these.

- Consider your personal view on the topic. Do you disagree/ agree or have an impartial view?

- Take a minute to PLAN what you are going to say in your answer.

- Think of the main idea you will introduce in each paragraph, then think of some supporting points.

- Before you start writing think about how you will introduce the topic.

- Do not copy he question!!!

- Introduce some arguments that are relevant to your own society or personal experience.

- Clearly state your conclusion, make sure that you address the question.

- Read through your answer when you have finished and check grammar spelling and punctuation.

- Check that you have liked your points together well.

- Make sure you have written enough words. Not less than 250!!!

When you have finished writing your report check what you have written by answering those questions:

- ☑ Is the length of the text appropriate?

- ☑ Does the text answer the question?

- ☑ Are there any common mistakes in the text? If so, what are they?

- ☑ Is there any repetition of words or phrases?

- ☑ Is anything missing?

- ☑ Are the paragraphs well linked together? If so, in what way?

- ☑ Does the report contain a wide range of vocabulary and structures?

www.idmadrid.es

Chapter 6: 101 IELTS Writing Grammar Rules

1. The word "people" is ALWAYS plural.

People are always talking about him (NOT People is...)

The people in the room were starting to get nervous. (NOT: The people in the room was...)

2. After would rather, use an infinitive (without to) or a past tense, not a present tense.

I'd rather stay at home this evening. (NOT I'd rather to stay at home...)

I would rather you paid me in cash. (NOT I would rather you pay me in cash.)

3. Use an -ing form after be/get used to.

I'm used to driving in London now, but it was hard at the beginning. (NOT I'm used to drive...)

I'll never get used to living in this place.

4. "How long are you here for?" Is a question about the future.

'How long are you here for?' 'Till Easter.' (NOT 'Since Christmas.')

5. Don't use could to talk about something that you succeeded in doing.

I managed to run 10 km yesterday in under an hour. (NOT I could run 10 km yesterday...)

How many eggs were you able to get? (NOT ...could you get?)

6. Indirect questions usually have the same construction as statements.

I asked where her parents were. (NOT USUALLY I asked where were her parents.)

The policeman wanted to know where I lived. (NOT ...where did I live?)

7. To say that something is not necessary, use needn't or don't have to, not mustn't.

You needn't pay now; tomorrow will be OK. (NOT You mustn't pay now; tomorrow will be OK.)

I don't have to wear a tie at work. (NOT I mustn't wear a tie at work.)

8. Everything is a singular word.

Everything was broken. (NOT Everything were broken.)

Is everything ready?

9. Use because or so, but not both together.

Because the train was late I missed the meeting. OR The train was late, so I missed the meeting. (BUT NOT Because the train was late, so I missed the meeting.)

10. We say something to a person.

She never says 'Hello' to me. (NOT She never says me 'Hello'.)

Andrew has said nothing to Peter. (NOT Andrew has said Peter nothing.)

11. Tell normally needs a personal object.

He told us that he was going home. (NOT He told that he was going home.)

I've told you everything I know.

12. Don't use every to talk about two people or things.

You can park on each side of the street. (NOT ...on every side of the street.)

He was holding a glass in each hand.

13. Far is unusual in affirmative sentences, except in a very formal style.

We live a long way from here. (NOT USUALLY We live far from here.)

It's a long way to Manchester.

14. We don't usually use before to mean 'in front of'.

You can park in front of the station. (NOT ... before the station.)

There's a big tree just in front of our house.

15. After look, we use at with an object.

Look at the moon! (NOT Look the moon!)

What are you looking at?

16. We use when, not as or while, to talk about ages and periods of life.

When I was 14 I first got interested in archaeology. (NOT As/While I was 14...)

We lived in London when I was a child. (NOT ... as/while I was a child.)

17. After as long as, use a present tense to refer to the future.

I'll remember this holiday as long as I live. (NOT ... as long as I will live.)

You can have my bike as long as you bring it back tomorrow.

18. We say as usual, not as usually.

Let's meet tomorrow at 10.00, as usual.

Vanessa late as usual.

19. As well as (with a similar meaning to 'not only... but also') is normally followed by an -ing form.

As well as breaking his leg, he hurt his arm. (NOT As well as he broke his leg...)

He works full time as well as bringing up three children.

20. Expressions like in three hours' time refer to the future.

We'll need the report in two weeks' time. (BUT NOT He wrote the report in four hours' time.)

I'll see you again in a month's time.

21. We don't normally use to after arrive.

What time do we arrive in London? (NOT … arrive to London?)

The train arrived at our station half an hour late.

22. Because is a conjunction; because of is a preposition.

We cancelled the match because it rained. (NOT … because of it rained.)

We cancelled the match because of the rain. (NOT …because the rain.)

23. After the verb lack, no preposition is necessary.

The soup lacks salt. (NOT … lacks of salt.)

It's a good novel, but it lacks structure.

24. Before (meaning 'before that') follows an expression of time.

Last summer, I decided to go and visit the town that I had left eight years before. (NOT … before eight years.)

I had already met her once, about three years before.

25. News is singular and uncountable

All the news is bad. (NOT All the news are bad.)

I have some news for you (NOT I have a news for you)

26. You borrow something from somebody.

I borrowed the money from my brother. (NOT I borrowed my brother the money.)

Can we borrow some sugar from you?

27. We prefer closed, not shut, before a noun.

When I talk to you, I feel as if I'm standing in front of a closed door. (NOT … a shut door.)

He's got a closed mind. You can't tell him anything.

28. We say come from (present) to give our town, country etc of origin.

James comes from Liverpool. (NOT James came from Liverpool.)

Where do you come from?

29. Comparatives are made with more or -er, but never both.

The weather is getting colder. (NOT ... more colder.)

Please try to be more polite. (NOT ... more politer.)

30. We never use on the contrary to give another side of a question.

It's hard work. On the other hand, it's interesting. (NOT on the contrary, it's interesting.)

She's very bad-tempered. On the other hand, she's generous.

31. In affirmative sentences we generally use a long time, not long, except in a very formal style.

We waited a long time, but she didn't come. (NOT We waited long, but ...)

It will be a long time before we invite her again.

32. Use superlatives to compare people and things with the groups that they belong to.

Sandra is the tallest of the five girls. (NOT Sandra is the taller of the five girls.)

I think I'm the oldest person in the class.

33. We often use in after dressed to describe the clothes

She was dressed in yellow from head to foot. She looked like a daffodil.

The bride was dressed in white silk.

34. We don't use it ... + infinitive with allow.

Smoking is not allowed. (NOT It is not allowed to smoke.)

We weren't allowed to use calculators in the exam. (NOT It wasn't allowed to use ...)

35. Whose means 'who is' or 'who has'; whose is a possessive.

Who's that? (NOT Whose that?)

Who's taken my keys? (NOT Whose taken my keys?)

Whose coat is that? (NOT Who's coat is that?)

36. We don't usually use other with uncountable nouns.

Can I have more rice? (NOT ... other rice?)

Perhaps we should use different oil. (NOT ... other oil.)

37. We use either, not any, to talk about two people or things.

I can write with either hand. (NOT ... with any hand.)

'Do you prefer Monday or Tuesday?' 'Either day will do.'

38. Don't put articles and possessives together before nouns.

She's a friend of mine. OR She's my friend. (BUT NOT She's a my friend.)

Peter's lost his keys. (NOT … the his keys.)

39. We say that somebody is good, bad, clever etc at something.

My sister is very good at Science. (NOT … good in Science.)

I'm very bad at languages.

40. Don't leave out a/an in negative expressions.

Don't got out without a coat. (NOT … without coat.)

It's difficult to get there if you haven't got a bike. (NOT … if you haven't got bike.)

41. We use any, not every, to say 'one or another'.

'Which newspaper would you like?' 'It doesn't matter. Any one.' (NOT … every one.)

'When would you like to come to dinner?' 'Any day is OK.'

42. Advice is uncountable.

Can you give me some advice? (NOT … an advice?)

My father gave me three pieces of advice. (NOT … three advices.)

43. We don't use some if we know the exact number.

You've got beautiful fingers. (NOT … some beautiful fingers.)

A mountain bike needs to have strong wheels. (NOT … some strong wheels.)

44. We don't use articles in some common expressions with home, school and bed.

Why isn't Angela at school today? (NOT … at the school today?)

I want to spend a day in bed.

45. When which? what? or who? are subjects, we make questions without do.

Which costs more - the blue one or the grey one? (NOT Which does cost more …?)

What happened to your bike? (NOT What did happen to your bike?)

Who phoned? (NOT Who did phone?)

46. We don´t use articles after the amount/number of.

I was surprised by the amount of money that was collected. (NOT … the amount of the money …)

The number of unemployed rose sharply last month. (NOT The number of the unemployed…)

47. We use because, not as or since, if the reason is the most important part of the sentence.

Why am I leaving? I'm leaving because I'm fed up. (NOT I'm leaving as/since I'm fed up.)

They're laughing because they think your hat's funny.

48. Travel is normally uncountable.

I like travel.

We went on a trip/journey to the Antarctic last spring. (NOT We went on a travel …)

49. Can has no infinitive. We use be able to instead.

I'd like to be able to sing. (NOT … to can sing.)

When will you be able to meet us?

50. The difference between a and an depends on pronunciation, not spelling.

She's a US citizen. (NOT She's an US citizen.)

Would you like to be an MP? (NOT ... a MP?)

51. Weather is uncountable.

We had terrible weather last week. (NOT ... a terrible weather ...)

I hope we get good weather at the weekend.

52. Words like President, King, Doctor in titles have no article.

President Obama visited the Pope. (NOT The President Obama ...)

I'd like to see Dr Jones. (NOT ... the Dr Jones.)

53. We usually use over, not across, to mean 'on/to the other side of something high'.

Why are you climbing over that wall? (NOT … across that wall?)

I threw his keys over the fence, where he couldn't get them.

54. Actually means 'really' or 'in fact', not 'now'.

She said she was 18, but actually she was 15.

In 1700 the population of London was higher than it is now. (NOT … than it actually is.)

55. Asleep and afraid are not normally used before nouns.

He had the innocent expression of a sleeping baby. (NOT … of an asleep baby.)

In the house, we found a frightened child hiding in the kitchen. (NOT … an afraid child.)

56. We don't usually put an adverb and its complement together before a noun.

We're looking for people who are skilled in design. (NOT … skilled in design people.)

He has a difficult accent to understand. (NOT … a difficult to understand accent.)

57. Eventually means 'finally', not ´from time to time´, 'possibly' or 'perhaps'.

It took a long time, but eventually he finished his studies.

I'm not sure what I'll do next year. Perhaps I'll go to university if I can get a place. (NOT Eventually I'll go to university …)

58. We don't usually use too before adjective + noun.

The problem was too difficult. (BUT NOT It was a too difficult problem.)

I put down the bag because it was too heavy. (BUT NOT I put down the too heavy bag.)

59. We usually put descriptive adjectives before classifying adjectives.

An old political idea (NOT A political old idea)

The latest educational reform (NOT The educational latest reform)

60. Nouns referring to nationality are often different from the corresponding adjectives.

Graham is typical Welshman. (NOT ... a typical Welsh.)

He's married to a Spaniard. (NOT ... a Spanish.)

61. Adjectives that express opinions usually come before other descriptive adjectives.

a lovely cool drink (NOT a cool lovely drink)

their wonderful old house (NOT their old wonderful house)

62. Pronoun objects come before adverb particles.

Can you switch it on, please? (NOT ...switch on it...)

I'm going to throw them all out. (NOT ... throw out them all.)

63. Adverbs can't usually be used instead of adjectives.

She danced happily into the room. (NOT She danced happy …)

I'm terribly sorry. (NOT I'm terrible sorry.)

64. After all doesn't mean 'finally'. It means 'all things considered' or 'in spite of what was expected'.

It took a long time, but finally we found our dream house. (NOT … but after all we found our dream house.)

She can make her own bed. After all, she's not a baby any more.

I expected to fail the exam, but I passed after all.

65. Ago comes after an expression of time.

Ann phoned two hours ago. (NOT … ago two hours.)

I should have finished this work six weeks ago.

66. We don't normally use all without a noun to mean 'everybody'.

Everybody was quiet. (NOT All were quiet.)

I've written to everybody. (NOT I've written to all.)

67. In exclamations with how, the adjective or adverb comes immediately after how.

How cold it is! (NOT How it is cold!)

How well she sings! (NOT How she sings well!)

68. We don't use every with uncountable nouns.

I like all music. (NOT I like every music.)

I can do every kind of work. (NOT ... every work.)

69. After either, we use a singular noun.

I can come on Wednesday or Thursday - either day is OK. (NOT ... either days ...)

She can write with either hand.

70. We usually ask 'What colour …?' without a preposition.

What colour is your new bike? (NOT Of what colour …?)

What colour is her hair this week?

71. We don't usually drop nouns after adjectives.

Poor little boy! (NOT Poor little!)

The most important thing is to be happy. (NOT The most important is to be happy.)

72. All day doesn't mean the same as every day.

I worked all day yesterday, from 8.00 till bedtime.

I worked every day except Sunday last week. (NOT … all day except Sunday …)

73. Don't drop a/an after what in exclamations.

What a rude man! (NOT What rude man!)

What an awful film! (NOT What awful film!)

74. Experience and experiment don't mean the same.

We did an experiment in the chemistry lesson to see if you could get chlorine gas from salt. (NOT We did an experience …)

I'm experimenting with a new perfume.

I had a lot of interesting experiences during my year in Africa. (NOT I had a lot of interesting experiments …)

Have you ever experienced the feeling that you were going mad? (NOT Have you ever experimented the feeling …?)

75. We don't usually use reflexive pronouns after feel.

I feel really energetic today. (NOT I feel myself really …)

Andrew often feels depressed. (NOT … feels himself depressed.)

76. We use half without of in expressions of measurement and amount.

They live about half a mile from here. (NOT ... half of a mile ...)

I only need half a pint.

77. We use hear, not listen to, to say that something 'comes to our ears'.

Suddenly I heard a strange noise. (NOT Suddenly I listened to a strange noise.)

Did you hear that?

78. After help, we can use object + infinitive (with or without to).

Can you help me (to) find my ring? (NOT ... help me finding my ring?)

Let me help you (to) wash up.

79. We usually say hope ...not, rather than do not hope.

I hope it doesn't rain tomorrow. (NOT I don't hope it rains tomorrow.)

'Is Peter coming this evening?' 'I hope not.'

80. We say that you crash into something.

Granny crashed into a tree yesterday. (NOT Granny crashed against a tree yesterday.)

The plane crashed into a mountain.

81. Singular forms are used before nouns in plural measuring expressions.

I found a ten-euro note on the pavement. (NOT ... a ten-euros note ...)

He goes for a five-mile walk every morning.

82. It's means 'it is' or 'it has'; its is a possessive.

It's late. (NOT Its late.)

It's stopped raining. (NOT Its stopped raining.)

The dog hasn't eaten its food. (NOT …it's food.)

83. We don't usually use also in short answers.

'I like this place.' 'Me too.' (NOT I also.)

'I've got a headache.' 'So have I.' (NOT I have also.)

84. We don't usually put a comma before that (conjunction or relative pronoun).

I knew that I had seen him somewhere before. (NOT I knew, that …)

She couldn't find the paper that had his address on. (NOT … the paper, that had …)

85. Rest (meaning 'things left over') is uncountable.

I'll take these grapes and you can have the rest. (NOT … the rests.)

We're having left-overs for supper. (NOT We're having rests …)

86. Same is normally used with the, and followed by as.

Give me the same again, please. (NOT Give me same again, please.)

She has the same birthday as me. (NOT She has my same birthday. OR She has same birthday like me.)

87. After would like, we normally use a -to infinitive.

Would you like to dance? (NOT Would you like dancing?)

I'd like to go to Australia. (NOT I'd like going to Australia.)

88. We use remind (of) to mean 'make somebody remember'.

Remind me to pay the milkman. (NOT Remember me to pay …)

The smell of hay reminds me of my childhood. (NOT … remembers me my childhood.)

For more details, see Practical English Usage Third Edition 499.

89. After accuse, we normally use of, not for.

She accused me of reading her letters. (NOT … for reading her letters.)

Both the young men are accused of attempted murder.

90. We don't normally use an infinitive after why.

I know how to do it, and I know when to do it, but I don't know why I should do it. (NOT … I don't know why to do it.)

Why do we lock this office?

91. Demonstratives replace articles.

I don't like that colour. (NOT … the that colour.)

Have you seen this report? (NOT … the this report.)

92. We don't normally use progressive forms of hear.

I (can) hear the sea. (NOT I am hearing the sea.)

I think I (can) hear Peter coming up the stairs.

93. After discuss, no preposition is necessary.

We spent half an hour discussing the weather. (NOT ... discussing about the weather.)

Let's discuss your plans.

94. We usually drop at in questions beginning What time ...?

What time would you like to eat? (NOT USUALLY At what time ...?)

I'm not sure what time the film starts.

95. We say on holiday (singular).

I'll be on holiday next week. (NOT ... on holidays ...)

We met John and Virginia when we were on holiday in Greece.

96. Don't drop a before hundred.

Our family has lived here for a hundred years. (NOT ... for hundred years.)

The factory is about a hundred miles west of London.

97. If you can't see or find somebody, they are nowhere to be seen/found.

When I went back to the car park, my car was nowhere to be seen. (NOT … my car was nowhere to see.)

The children were nowhere to be found. (NOT … nowhere to find.)

98. We don't normally use might to talk about past possibility.

I felt very hot and thirsty. Perhaps I was ill. (NOT … I might be ill.)

I saw a girl going into Peter's house. Maybe it was Jeanne. (NOT … It might be Jeanne.)

99. We use beat, not win, to say that one person defeats another in a game, fight etc.

My girlfriend beat me at poker last night. (NOT My girlfriend won me at poker last night.)

Aberdeen beat Bristol 3-0.

100. We use even, not also, to add surprising information.

They were all asleep, even the guard dog. (NOT … also the guard dog.)

Everybody was in time, even Granny. (NOT …also Granny.)

101. Was vs. were

"If I were rich, I'd buy lots and lots of shoes." (NOT … If I was rich …..)

This mistake is so common among native speakers of English that it is commonly acceptable to say was and it is even quite possible that the examiners won't notice.

If what you're saying is hypothetical, then you need to use were. If you've used "if," that's a pretty good indicator that were is appropriate.

"I wouldn't go there if I were you."

(You're not me, so it's subjunctive)

or

"If I were at home right now, I'd be watching a film."

LINKING MARKERS

ADDITION

In addition [to NP], ...

Moreover, ...

Also, ...

Apart from [NP], ...

Furthermore, ...and ...

not only ...,

but also ...   , who...

, which...

, where...

, when...

CONTRAST

However, ...

Nevertheless, ...

On the other hand, ...

In contrast, ...

In spite of [NP], ...

Despite [NP], ... but ...

...(and) yet...   although...

whereas...

while...

in spite of the fact that...

despite the fact that...

CAUSE/

EFFECT

So...

As a result...

Consequently...

Therefore...

Thus...

Hence...

For this reason...

Because of [NP],...   ...(and) so...

...(and) hence...   so...

so that...

because...

due to the fact that...

POSITIVE

CONDITION

In that case,...

If so,...

Then,...   ...and...

...and (then)...   if...

as/so long as...

CHOICE/

NEGATIVE

CONDITION   Alternatively, ...

Otherwise,...

Instead of [NP],...

Rather than [NP],...

If not,...   ...or (else)...   If... not...

unless...

TIME ORDER/

LISTING

Then...

Afterwards,...

First(ly),...

Second(ly),...

Next,...

Prior to [NP],...

Before [NP],...

Finally / Lastly,...   ...(and (then)... before...

after...

, after which...

when...

now that...

Exercise 1

Rewrite the information below as TWO or THREE sentences. You must decide how the ideas are logically related and then use a marker or conjunction (coordinating or subordinating) to match your meaning.

Learning French is not easy.

Many people would argue that learning Spanish is harder.

French and English share a lot of similarities in their vocabulary.

French and Spanish both have different articles for masculine and feminine nouns.

You have to change the endings of adjectives to match the nouns.

This is hard for speakers of English.

English does not use adjective endings.

Most people believe that speaking English helps you to start learning French and Spanish.

When you have passed the basic stages, English is less helpful.

At an advanced level of Spanish and French, knowing English is arguably not very helpful.

Answers:

Learning French is not easy, but many people would argue that learning Spanish is harder, because French and English share a lot of similarities in their vocabulary. Nevertheless, French and Spanish both have different articles for masculine and feminine nouns. Therefore, you have to change the endings of adjectives to match the nouns, which is hard for speakers of English since English does not use adjective endings. Most people believe that speaking English helps you to start learning French and Spanish but when you have passed the basic stages, English is less helpful and at an advanced level of Spanish and French, knowing English is arguably not very helpful.

Vocabulary Exercises for IELTS Preparation

Exercise 1:

Complete each of the following sentences by supplying the correct form of the word in brackets. There are FIFTEEN questions in all.

1) I can't thank you enough. The support you've given us both has been .... (MEASURE)

2) Politicians must always ensure they give a .... response to any sensitive questions. (MEASURE)

3) The designer came and took lots of .... around the office. (MEASURE)

4) The judge was forced to call the trial to an end and let the accused go free because of a legal .... (TECHNICAL)

5) Well, ... speaking, I shouldn't allow you to leave the room during an examination. (TECHNICAL)

6) Can you call the .... and ask him to come up and have a look at my computer? (TECHNICAL)

7) She made a very good .... during her visit and hopes to create closer links with the company. (IMPRESS)

8) He's a very .... young man who is easily influenced by others. (IMPRESS)

9) The team played really well and the captain was particularly .... (IMPRESS)

10) Despite the initial problems the machine is now fully .... (OPERATE)

11) Having looked at your X-Ray I'm afraid to say your condition is .... You will just have to live with the pain. (OPERATE)

12) The patient is in a stable condition and is now on the .... table. (OPERATE)

13) You can't do three jobs at once. That's totally .... (PRACTICE)

14) You're .... old enough to drive. Why don't you think about saving up for lessons? (PRACTICE

15) You need to .... regularly if you want to improve. (PRACTICE)

Answer Key

1) I can't thank you enough. The support you've given us both has been .... (MEASURE)

Immeasurable

2) Politicians must always ensure they give a .... response to any sensitive questions. (MEASURE)

measured

3) The designer came and took lots of .... around the office. (MEASURE)

measurements

4) The judge was forced to call the trial to an end and let the accused go free because of a legal .... (TECHNICAL)

technicality

5) Well, ... speaking, I shouldn't allow you to leave the room during an examination. (TECHNICAL)

technically

6) Can you call the .... and ask him to come up and have a look at my computer? (TECHNICAL)

technician

7) She made a very good .... during her visit and hopes to create closer links with the company. (IMPRESS)

impression

8) He's a very .... young man who is easily influenced by others. (IMPRESS)

impressionable

9) The team played really well and the captain was particularly .... (IMPRESS)

impressive

10) Despite the initial problems the machine is now fully .... (OPERATE)

operational

11) Having looked at your X-Ray I'm afraid to say your condition is .... You will just have to live with the pain. (OPERATE)

inoperable

12) The patient is in a stable condition and is now on the .... table. (OPERATE)

operating

13) You can't do three jobs at once. That's totally .... (PRACTICE)

impractical

14) You're .... old enough to drive. Why don't you think about saving up for lessons? (PRACTICE)

practically

15) You need to .... regularly if you want to improve. (PRACTICE)

Practice

About the Author

MARC ROCHE is from Manchester originally and currently lives in Madrid with his wife Madilyn and his son Macson. Marc is a teacher, trainer, writer and business manager. He has collaborated with organizations such as the British Council, the Royal Melbourne Institute of Technology and University of Technology Sydney among others. Marc has also worked with multinationals such as Nike, GlaxoSmithKline or Bolsas y Mercados. In his free time, he likes to travel, cook, write, play sports, watch football (Manchester City and Real Madrid) and spend time with friends and family.

Learn more about Marc at <u>amazon.com/author/marcroche</u>

Learn more about Marc's Training Company at <u>https://www.idmadrid.es/</u>

Make sure to look the free training resources for students and teachers at https://www.idmadrid.es/recursos.html

Other books by Marc Roche

IELTS WRITING: ADVANCED WRITING MASTERCLASS (IELTS TASKS 1 & 2): IELTS ACADEMIC WRITING BOOK BAND 7.0 - 8.5

101 Grammar Rules for IELTS: Instant Study Notes (IELTS Grammar)

Legal English: Contract Law: Basic to Advanced TOLES (Legal English and TOLES Preparation Book 1)

ONE LAST THING... (A VERY SPECIAL REQUEST)

If you enjoyed this book or found it useful I'd be very grateful if you'd post a short review on Amazon. Your support really does make a difference and I read all the reviews personally so I can get your feedback and make this book even better.

If you'd like to leave a review then all you need to do is click the review link on this book's page on Amazon here:

Thanks again for your support and good luck in the exam!

Made in the USA
Lexington, KY
23 February 2019